C0-AYQ-241

POEMS FOR THE PARDONED

Also by Cathryn Hankla

POETRY

Phenomena (1983)

Afterimages (1991)

Cool Water (chapbook, 1992)

Negative History (1997)

Texas School Book Depository (2000)

Emerald City Blues (2002)

FICTION

Learning the Mother Tongue (1987)

A Blue Moon in Poorwater (1988; reprint 1998)

POEMS FOR THE PARDONED

CATHRYN HANKLA

Louisiana State University Press

Baton Rouge

2002

Copyright © 1982, 1984, 1996, 2000, 2001, 2002 by Cathryn Hankla
All rights reserved
Manufactured in the United States of America
First printing

Cloth: 11 10 09 08 07 06 05 04 03 02   Paper: 11 10 09 08 07 06 05 04 03 02
       5 4 3 2 1   5 4 3 2 1

Designer: Laura Roubique Gleason
Typeface: Minion
Printer and binder: Thomson-Shore, Inc.

Library of Congress Cataloging-in-Publication Data:

Hankla, Cathryn, 1958–
  Poems for the Pardoned / Cathryn Hankla.
    p. cm.
  ISBN 0-8071-2812-0 (cloth : alk. paper) — ISBN 0-8071-2813-9
(pbk. : alk. paper)
  I. Title.
  PS3558.A4689 P64 2002
  811'.54—dc21

2002003597

The author offers grateful acknowledgment to the editors of the following publications,
in which some of the poems herein originally appeared, sometimes in a slightly different
form: ALCA-Lines: Journal of the Assembly on the Literature and Culture of Appalachia:
"The Consolation of Mountains" and "Indian Pipe"; Denver Quarterly: "Collaboration";
Images: "Marred"; Mississippi Valley Review: "Mirrors"; Parnassus Literary Journal:
"Attaching an Arm"; Shenandoah: "On Athena's Shoulder."

"Dancers at the Edge" first appeared in The Sacred Place: Witnessing the Holy in the
Physical World, ed. W. Scott Olsen and Scott Cairns, University of Utah Press, 1996.

The paper in this book meets the guidelines for permanence and durability of the
Committee on Production Guidelines for Book Longevity of the Council on Library
Resources.♾

Contents

POEMS FOR THE PARDONED

On Athena's Shoulder

The owl's cat eyes echoed the highbeams
and I swerved. I knew nothing more.
It must have lighted on the country road
some time before. I took the last curve

and dipped down a slope
where I had once spun on ice,
end over beginning, like a planet
toppled in the tilt of seasons.

Hearing, still, the voices of the evening
and my own erratic wisdom
looping in my inner ear, I almost missed
the horned owl swiveling to confront me

with its white throat. All of the words
in my head turned, then, into owls.
At the center of every question hunched
a silent owl, a silent way of knowing.

And I was left wondering
whether field mouse or broken wing
had downed it there, wondering who
would come along and hit it square.

Dead Dog

As rain raises a tin voice
against roofs and stranded leaves
pelt pounded ground, outside
the window I know the red dog
still lies on its back, exposing
black teats, sucked dry.

Encountering the lone dog, I raised
my stick, remembering the pack that once
attacked my terrier and me, that formed
a functional circle from which first
one and then the next dog
lunged to catch fur or skin
in teeth. I've scars to bear from this,
so when the red dog sniffed
tentatively and blinked a swollen
eye toward me, I felt
a subtle mastery over memories
of my fear, risen like wood smoke
in the specter of the red dog, its neck
ruffed in tough red fur,
some dominant gene of the chow
emerging in this gentle mongrel.
Beggar's lice matted the bushy
mast of its tail; the haunches showed
skeletal signs of hunger. I wondered
whether its recent whelps had hastened
the fate that dumped the red dog
to fend along an unfamiliar
stretch of country mile and then
to rest just the other side
of barbed wire, down an embankment
below the road I walk most
days, my dog pulling me
behind like a faithful, ill-fitting
shadow.

We saw the red dog

twice more before noting
its absence and its stench in one moment
from two senses in synch, my dog
tugging me over the shoulder
before I pulled him up
short of corpus and barbs. Regrouped,
perched like owls or hawks, we searched
from the height of the road, we studied
the position of the red dog sprawled
on its back with head twisted to one
side and belly undefended, open
to the sky. A sickness turned inside
my stomach. Although I'd observed
no bullet holes, I wondered
how, if hit by a car, the dog
had wound up on the other side
of the fence to die.

     Had I
wished the red dog dead,
in a minute of fear, releasing the thought
like a genie to do my bidding?
Anyone would say this
is impossible, and yet I
know that thoughts can harm
as surely as heal at a distance. I
loved my dog more as we walked,
and yet at four A.M.
I looked into the bathroom mirror,
deep into eyes inseparable from a killer's.

In less than twenty-four hours
I walk the road again and see,
festooned on a branch, raised like
the Jolly Roger, a deerskin
complete with white tail, below
it the pared rib cages of three
kindred, scattered hoofs and entrails

dumped out of season on the most convenient
ground, rolled from a truck until
they hit the fence to rot.

Five years I've walked this stretch
of road; five years I've seen
this same macabre effect created
by soulless cheaters who treat
these deaths as sport and leave their
stink to putrefy the air.
Again, I know just how
it feels to wish one's enemies
would suffer painfully.
And I've not seen the worst
of the changes out here. A few
more steps, short-leashing
my dog, who has caught the scent of blood,
then I cast my eyes over
the bank to the red dog's plot.
There, I see her contorted
on her back minus her lion's mane
and head. No beast but man would wield
such disrespect upon the dead.
I revive the terrors I've read
or seen in photographs: heads
posted on sticks as deterrents, mass
graves exhumed, whole lineages
marched to quick extinction, enlisted
women routinely raped by fellow
soldiers, a town like Lidice
erased in conflagration.

                                        If
I roam too far it is not
merely to shock. Could special
circumstances explain each
atrocity we know by heart?

Two women in love—trained
wilderness and hiking guides—
were murdered. Unsolved. This week
a woman working late was found
tied to her office chair, throat
cut. I cannot picture any
beast but one finding fun
in beheading a bloated dog. The black
teats exercise a hypnotic
hold. I want to find just one
motley reddish life—escaped,
perhaps, from the weight of a drowning sack—
and carry it home in my arms.

Dancers at the Edge

I've grown used to the ones
who wander close, brave
with velvet antlers, who sneak up
when I'm raking leaves,
reading, or planting bulbs.
We eye each other, theirs
darker, more reflective
than mine. These creatures,
wild and new to this world,
do not flinch at human
scent. I will teach them
distance, prepare them for
November guns. I clap
my hands, bang plastic pots
and wait for them to run.

Two dancers entwine tawny necks,
bow to taste wild mushrooms.
The poison is all in my head.

Indian Pipe

Thinking "mushroom," I plucked the bird's-nest roots'
Pale, umbilical stems before their bowed,
Translucent heads could bloom. No herbalist
Would have confused the two, doubted

The potency of this juice for stinging
Eyes and root for sleep. Indian pipe grows
Infrequently on wooded slopes where slow
Changes can take hold without our knowing

And wildflowers can be colorless, odd
Albinos, rare as *agape* in a world
Of eros. Where will we have to live,
The two of us, controlled only by love?

What leaf-strewn shade will nurture us until
Our scalelike leaves unfurl, longings fulfill?

Digging Tulips, Watching
Ducks on the Fall Equinox

The human mind must wallow in the mud
as ducks float by, paddling forward
on undetected strength.
Ducks plod the currents
and make it look like gliding.
Ducks tend to blend together.
I am beginning
to understand deception in the least
of things, how it propels, eddies,
bends to mean:
I spend my life
on what is missing, walk
a circuit marked by only subtle signs,
allow my eyes to waver
over messages left in twigs,
footprints. I never know enough.

I trust my fingers in the dirt
to bring up rocks and roots,
to thin the bed, upending bulbs.
Tulip earth tracks through my chest.
I try to stifle the cough.

Resemblances

A delta, tributaries
seen from above,
branches like the roots of a tree.

The white mask of a cow's face,
like bones beneath
bleached free of any fleshly trace.

Sea urchins release white sperm,
smear eggs like stars
into a spiral galaxy.

Fractals endlessly repeat
the whole in parts
only unfocused eyes can meet.

Nature favors likenesses,
mirroring you
and me, our puzzling kisses.

Space

Space, like time, engenders forgetfulness. . . .
—Thomas Mann

A clear space, the mitered corner
inside a drawer where worn boards meet.

Sharp pieces of mirror stacked beside shells,
but the corner is empty,
                        empty and small,
the top corner of an envelope, saved.

This space could be measured
as from ceiling to adjoining wall.

It could be fought over
or by all accounts forgotten.

A clear space, triangles of air
between open fingers, perfect windows
that can shut like slats on a blind.

A corner assignation, air
erasing an angle of sense.

By degrees of separation,
absence defines a love of space.

Mirrors

Windsocks stiffen, inflate and rotate
in any direction. I was driving
to the town airport, watching these serpents
switch in the distance of a field,
when a man fell out of the sky.
I saw the top of his head
in the rearview mirror
as he dashed to ground.
I turned around.

Dressed in white, ribbons of luminous
tethers, light streaming
through stained glass across his back,
he waved me down and asked for a lift.
He had trouble stowing his cloud
at his feet. He opened the vent
and held the door ajar.
I heard wind whistle as I drove,
not very far.

When he left my car at the runway's end,
I saw his buckle flash
as the sun caught it flush.
I saw my face reflected,
as if bent in the hollow of a spoon.
He said he was going up again,
he loved the rush.
I wondered where he might touch down,
maybe the moon.

A Portrait of the Spacewoman

This woman, who has never watched herself
button a blouse, serves as a camera

launched to ponder itself.
This woman slips into dresses

the painter waits to photograph.
He won't paint straight from life

but adds or subtracts
crows'-feet in her future or past,

the mole above her left eye,
stained fingertips from pitting sour fruit.

This woman sheaths her curves in silk.
The painter may depict her in a poodle skirt

or a space suit, paint
her drowsy eyes a suspect blue,

recall her collision with a static
family tree, effects invisible now,

that turned half of her
third grade face into bark. Or

he may evoke the clownish red cheeks
that plagued her latter youth.

She monitors her ship, reflects on sex
with her grounded husband, remembers

the Christmas when her best friend
received the Visible Man

and she the Visible Woman.
They mated minus the usual mess.

The baby was never born but lived
as a specimen beneath a plastic dome

latticed with red nail polish.
Even this, a brushfire of desire

well within her control.
Coast-to-coast, by satellite,

the spacewoman waves to parents
and husband, and misses

the Mexican jumping bean her copilot
sends toward her nose.

We cannot stop looking at her,
but vanishing is what she craves,

a cool illusion draped like space around her
to obscure her from our gaze.

Attaching an Arm

The doctors came at you from all sides
Armed with the tools of their craft.
You lay on the gurney, eyes masked
From the theater's glare. Looking
Up, you confronted your own darkness
As if you were locked in a box. The doctors
Opened the ice chest and lifted the stranger's
Elbow and every wish you wanted to command.

Days after the operation you would stare
At the hand, waiting for it to open.

The Way Window Frames

My thoughts have flailed in logic's
nets. I ache, stretch neck
to test the hours' damage on the spine,
pretend I air more than my eye
where snaking limbs bear green
blotches of spring. I stroke
the ratiné of bark, fret up
brief buds (before they open,
spun from dark),
the way my wheels must always slow
for yellow bands where children jump.

This rain, over time,
has drowned our sense of voice,
of laugh, whisper, rasp,
and every greening touch. It must
have been a constant, like the night,
berating dreams, before I grasped your hand,
cipher, and sang as if into a cup
of breath inside a well
where brave children fell into their fears
and gravity dispelled.

When You Die, They Bring Mirrors

As a child
I studied the signs of the deaf,
but when my father died
he took with him my hands.

He speaks, but I am underwater,
listening for gusts that carry him.
Mute, I eat, raise crumbs,
manna for animals' mouths.
Dreaming of flight, of journeys,
I drink in the sea, gulping salt.

Day empties a catalog of departures.
Lamplight splashes, a far-off
slapping of surf on sand.
My flat face turns from the sun.
Shadows form as tight as fingernails,
lungs sift breath from sleep, and
my head cracks like a shell,
exhaling nightmares of land.

I leave the pool drained,
transfused with foreign liquid,
breathe steam through open pores,
rising dizzy, remembering:
knuckles floating up through water
thick and warm as blood,
elbows that rose afterward
submerging fingertips.

When you die, they place shiny coins
on your eyes. When you die,
they bring mirrors—
check to see which parts are missing.
A cage casts over your body. Sky breaks
open sails, and there is singing. They chisel
ice, kick the chips away like bits of bone.

Train sound woke me,
its whistle lay me down to sleep.
His gloved hand waved
from the wheel as he sped by.
When we moved to another town, twin tracks
separated me from the earless engineer.
And I wanted to lose the world
of sound to be like him.

I remember lime luna moths, sleeping
ghosts against the glass of my father's coach.

I see a dragon pitcher
and twelve seahorse cups. I feel
the breeze that blew through the passage
when the owl flew from its cage.

Wax warms for unwritten letters, sealing
them away. Thank you notes for every
day will never be enough.

You pass him on the rails, someone
you know but have not yet met.
Turn your eye—tomorrow
you will go in search, to offer one last gift.

Luna

Sliding open the doorway to my house,
I let in lime green Luna's pendulous
Wings that wax and wane in tremulous swings
From ceiling to floor. I douse fast the lights
Inside and flick the floods, hoping Luna
Will flutter to glass, hang there, wait. Dusted
Wings are fragile things, and touching them means
Uncertainties, effects of life or death
Wrought by pure desires to help nature
Become nature, to keep ambiguous
Boundaries clear from creature to creature.
Luna flies out, and I exhale, then catch
A breath: she flings herself back through the slot,
Into my hands of longing and release.

On the summer solstice, sated from touch,
I wake to my cyclical blood and ache.
As I wipe away the signs, I hear
Rattling heartbeats of Luna's wings against
The bathroom screen, as if in a battle
Of wills with me, strangely attracted yet
Free.

Riparian Rites

It never works to muscle water.
I learned to be swamped early.

In the baby pool
I nearly drowned,

trying to reach a shiny quarter.
I kept my head above water

for years, yet made myself follow
Simon Says headfirst

down the slide. One night
a boy ripped his biceps from the bone,

scaling barbed wire to skinny-dip.
At summer camp, spring-fed liquid ice

shriveled every sex, turned
one easily into the other.

Everyone begins by floating,
as when a word becomes a name,

limbs enter and exit in rhythm.
Panting midwinter laps at the Y

for lifesaving class, I
was terrified of 12-foot dives

to haul up cinder blocks
said to resemble dead weight.

Weary of clearing mask and snorkel,
scared I was all form and no substance,

I couldn't help remembering the way
my parents screamed at each other

like there was no tomorrow. But usually
one arrived, and I did qualify

to teach children and middle-aged women—
who wanted dry faces at any cost—

to find their secret buoyancy.
One sloshed husband

pitched his wife, my weakest student,
into the deep end

where she battled surface tension
and thrashed her strong, forgotten legs,

shouting, "Save me!"
unmindful that she was swimming.

Limbo

This I admit is a place I have never
understood yet easily find, a space marked
free for those of us lost

between a little high water and clear,
open sky. It's always hard to say how I
got here, steered by my own lights,

buoyed by the idea of an honorable life.
And so I choose truth,
Knowing the choice brings no assurance

that I am right. Merely honest at the expense
of being kind, I tread water, barely
keeping my nose in the air.

Lips parched, face ulcerated from salt,
I bob apart. A fin pauses
in its circle, then aims for my heart.

Collaboration

In my family I've always wanted
to be the Black, Lesbian, Jew

with communist sympathies.
I've aspired to the democratic process.

On holidays we tend to eat together,
my family and I, despite the fact

that I am a single woman. It's amazing
what mashed potatoes and a crown roast

of pork can overlook. Some say
the way to a man's heart

is through his stomach.
Mine tends to grumble over too much

fat. I subsist on attitude alone—
maybe just a side dish of corn pudding

or pickled beets. I've been saving myself
for dessert. In the darkened

kitchen we have our tryst.
I take what's left of the pumpkin pie

and sit, relentlessly dipping
an heirloom fork. I cannot help

eating their food, these people
who raised me. It tastes good,

like childhood, when I was allowed
to bicycle free for hours

and never called home.

Truce

In chalky lines, I scrawled
tall words on rock walls
repeating dissolutions of soft shale
until my letters filled the slab
between the rains:

Lincoln Wept Here

Your Mother Cooks Socks in Hell

Jesus Slept

I rocked within our car,
holding my breath
when we drove past the words
I'd written,
hoping Mother never saw.

Home by Dark

Tell the mothers and the fathers
We will not be home on time—

Danger teased us
Down fast twists of slide.

We cannot retrace
Quick touches of deed

To dare
That drew us into dark.

We cannot return
Home to split-rails,

White lies we told
To keep the status quo.

Black Cat

The black cat crosses
right to left;
we lift our hats to spit.

Salt spills. We hunch
a shoulder to flick
the stuff, not shucking

responsibility to habit,
the pain in the neck of keeping up
with luck. We don't walk

under ladders here or
pass on stairs, one
going up, one buttering down

the bread. We don't toss hats lightly
on beds, or ignore an itching
palm. We don't miss

a trick, do anything for the hell
of it. We stick to the tried
and the true, one end of the margarine

if we can help it. End of October
and still no frost for pumpkins.
Tomatoes redden in Indian sun.

The *Farmer's Almanac* suggests the moon
for harvest and the fish
for planting.

Don't turn the calendar before
months end or open umbrellas here.
Don't leave the tree in your house

after New Year's. Be sure to make
a birthday wish. Bird-shaped maize,
bunched in three, hangs knocking

on our front door. Inside
we string beads by instinct
and turn the last square of quilt

askew, to honor unfounded
perfection, in a world
we don't yet understand.

Picture Your Ad Here

On this roadside sign
obscured by rust and vines

you might advertise
toilets that swirl

and swirl without a flush.
Your bad luck

at games of chance
and marriage

or the fact of fallen arches.
You might choose

to lure others to you
through a false display

of cheerful zest
by buying a new outfit

shirt-shoes-car
that she did not select.

When by yourself
tending house

you will need to decide
if a bad smell in the wall

balances the persistent
scratchings of a mouse.

You will need to decide
what to advertise.

House of Guilt

Here is the house that guilt built:
you worry that you paid too much

for sundeck, heat pump,
tired roof, and windows

that half work.
Even the shiny oak parquet

where beige carpet reigned
bears a decade of doggy redolence.

And a house must have floors, some
ground besides guilt to pace.

A dilemma of course,
but not of the first order.

After years you meet another love
who might have you

but who observes
your house is meant for one.

How can you explain the absence
of ample closets or dining room?

Your boudoir accommodates one person
lying sleepless in bed, staring up.

Admit what you must
and naturalize the feral parcel

with daffodils, perennials. Dig
a trench for exotic, towering tulips.

The soil is at least well drained.
Wait for color in the spring.

The Consolation of Mountains

She said, "Old as the hills," when you'd request
Your mother's age. "How old is that?" you asked,
Staring out to the ragged rim of rock,
Spare winter firs that greened a swath of air.

If actuary tables are complete,
You have not reached halfway and yet believe
That speaking of long sleep means you're awake,
That your heartbeat stays tuned to turning tides

Without an end. Conceived sea level, you
Were carried high, and by the time you dropped
Through water thick with your own weight of words,
The peaks of Appalachia shaped your world.

The sun, when you could see it breaking through,
Went down by four o'clock behind a thing
That cast its shadow over everyone,
That moved inside your house on moonlit nights

Like a humpbacked blessing or a curse. It
Formed a reason for most everything, from
Pokeweed ink and salad to abstractions
Like poverty and ignorance of books.

But when you visited the valley, you
Would ask about the blue unraveling
You glimpsed from certain angles in the car.
Comforted by the word *ridge,* rocked to sleep

By the least implication of mountains,
Your dreams floated you over a landscape
Flattened only by your inward flight.
What blocks, as these hills do a view, still

Offers revelation by teaching you to note
The sparse, subtle flowers growing wild.
All mountains have a name. The Blue Ridge
Range is not the same as the Alleghenies.

Bent, Mill, Tinker, Catawba, and Dead Man
Surround you, which means you make your home
In a valley, which means rivers, which means
You are not without interpretations

Or well-worn clichés for life. You are not,
Though, as shallow as you seem. Roots planted
Deep, yet you still seek the consolation
Of heights and drag yourself up rocky steeps.

First Desk

The vanity came down from the attic
wearing a coat of dust,
a candy-striped ruffle
tacked across her front.

I began by ripping off her skirt,
then sanded painted layers,
irritating white and green
and flesh, down to solid wood.

Linseed oil darkened the raw
surface, enriched its purpose.
On the support, I finally gave up—
too many nooks and bevels to strip

by hand. I bought a can of black
enamel and brushed it up to meet
the rich grain patience
had uncovered. At my inheritance

I worked. Facing a window,
not a mirror, I found the words.

Knockings

Blooming redbud against
    snow's sudden gust
brushed in beneath spring,
    a low, repetitive humming

where I thought I could step
    without sinking.
A dull knock, knocking
    of the woodpecker's red head,

thrusts of beak into waking wood
    and something you said,
without thinking that it could
    charm or sting, begs

a second guess.
    Ask the African woman
who gave birth in a tree
    how she feels about security.

Experiences alter us
    beyond what's believed.

Nine Days

We are bare. We are stripped to the bone
and we swim in tandem. . . .
    —Anne Sexton, "Eighteen Days Without You"

I pull the plug
on the hair dryer, exchange it for steam inhalation.
The dog barks to be let in—

I breathe tea tree and lavender oils,
drink ginger infusion. From Prague, Miriam suggests
boiled onions and honey for sore throat.

I try every cure,
                ingest garlic and juice,
peppermint tea, chicken soup.

        My tongue reeks of zinc.
My sponsor says, whatever you do,
don't call. I resist.

The left side of my face throbs like a rotten tooth.
        I can't forget
the instant we first met.

Light radiated from your upturned face
through irises, ionospheric.
Your bulky sweater draped

the small, warm shape I would trace with my mouth,
with every pore. I longed for you
as for irenic tides.

My sponsor says, whatever you do,
don't go back for more. Remember the long
curse of lying hand-tied and tongue-tied

as her spine arched away. Remember the misery of lost
sleep, when she left you for the better part of a year.
Remember when deep kisses turned to skimming.

Remember, remember
how crazy you felt.
Love is, I think. Love is nothing if not—

irate barking from the beloved, ignored dog,
rain thumps steady down the spouts—
                                        crazy. I

reach for the phone, dial
                    my doctor's number
to appeal for stronger drugs, conventional cures.

But the doctor is out.
The weekend stretches over me,
days like petals blown down a waterfall.

        Every day I remember
and every day I don't call.

Marred

Admit the apple and bite:
without hunger, I teethe
through scarred skin,
sink deep to find the seeded
questions. How does it feel
to core a human?

Your letters burn
almost completely,
though ashes mar the snow.
I strip your photo from the frame,
first searching
the half of your face you showed.

A Variation on the Roses of Saadi

This morning I wanted to bring you roses
but the tight knot in my throat
was like a belt tightened close
around my dress, my dress covered with roses.

This morning I wanted to bring you roses
but the knot burst, I said your name,
and petals flew in the wind, to follow waves,
painting them red with flame.

Tonight my dress carries your scent,
a fragrant souvenir. I breathe in
roses, think the knot in my chest might erupt
like the bud time could not restrain.

An Established Interior and a Close-Up

The window frames
Cornflower sea
The mirror a dark reflection
Of the chair's bent wood

Sunlight counterpoints
The empty pose of violin case
And the poised chair pulled
To face its image

In close-up the mirror's black surface
Ghost of self-contempt
Gives nothing back
To the anemones

Not even their own pink and white
Red and purple
Snaking from green deaths
Placated by water and vase

After Matisse's *Interior with a Violin Case* and
Anemones with a Black Mirror.

Something the Heart of the Rain Is Changing

I want to look out my window and see
Something that was not there before,
That goes beyond your mother,
My father, perhaps a waterfall
Where there was only barren ground,
Or a fence, to separate what we adopt
From what we refuse to become.

Outside my window, instead, pouring
In the rain, I see the names we call
Each other coming down: "Selfish,"
"Withdrawn," "Abandoner," "Deceiver."
These names are falling in the rain
In two voices, two independent clauses
chugging nowhere, to prove

A point that spears us both and nourishes
Neither. Outside the restaurant, the engine
Running on and on, we'd rather starve
Than go inside and hear the band's love songs,
Rather spend our hour, which could end
In a fraction, on rebuke and contempt,
On past accounts and charges left unpaid.

I dreamed I rushed along in a storm drain,
Trying to hold on to the mane of my dog,
Trying to keep his head above water,
Yet I sputtered down and came up without him,
And spent the rest of the dream searching
For the hairy face of the one dog
I loved, mistaking his face in the face

Of another, a dog with a gash
Beneath one eye, the wound I feared
My dog would have. But my dog was smart,
And someone said he had survived,
Had shaken the water from his fur and roamed
The refugee camp like a free man.
I wanted to believe he was looking for me.

Loving the Poor in Spirit

The poor are always with us,
Jesus said. But did he say that they
would look so much like us,
on certain days when the wind
lifts every hair on the head of the world
and sparrows fall without a trace?

Who covered your head with a hooded cape,
Victorian collar upturned
to obscure your face? Who took
the red cummerbund and too tightly sashed
your tender shape, so that
my touch sends you shuddering?

Who did this to you, who
rifled through the best of your
pages, left you in a twisted plot
of a little girl's saddest day?
Who told you to keep quiet,
whom must you defy and obey?

Betrayal

Inside New Jersey they found
Two cons discussing their childhoods with tears
In their eyes, saying how good they could
Have been, if only they'd had fathers.

Inside your apartment I found
The black bean bag I loaned you in 1975, the sack
Of lost buttons my aunt saved since
I was a child, the remains of the birthday cake
You said tasted so good it made you cry.
If only I had found the lava lamp.

Inside your heart because you led me there by the short hairs
I found BIG RED gum wrappers, a soiled wedding
Invitation, adoption papers I don't remember signing,
A map bearing notations on the most practical routes
Between anywhere and where you live.
If only I had found you there.

Inside the moon they found
A molten core that swirled and stewed
Like the fierce core of the earth but with
A crack, a broken record repeating, *if only, if only.*

Surgery

Because she might have died,
the surgeon took her under and kept her
longer and longer. An ancient
fish, she sprouted gills and scales, adapting
to a distant world, as I waited, thinking
everything I cared for on this earth
swam the anesthetized dark, learning
a way to survive alone. I had to learn
what I must risk by coupling. I kept coughing in
the same familiar air, trying to
reach a depth below trust in another
or oneself, a truth beneath the human bargains
that we strike in bed.

Because she did not die,
I faced again the loss of all I loved
and fled until my heart owned up to its own failing:
the abandoned heart goes numb, gives out, folds in
and tries to knit a sleeve through which to breathe.
I fell as silent in my sickness as she
beneath the knife that carved out inconclusion, left
a mark where I had covered her
with my heat and health and life, knowing I
gave little comfort. What price to pay
for knowledge, that old fall. In learning
how to reach through death
I lost all objects but love itself.

Cutting Losses

Sides splitting
with pain, I held my bladder under control
because the telephone rang.
                    I had imagined
contradictory scenarios: the inevitable call
dropped, like a commercial, into a TV show.
Driving my car I might mysteriously feel
the moment it happened before being told.
Or my husband would lean over me, hug me
with the truth, but not this
ridiculous trap of mind and body,
my mother's voice soothing my ear with news,
"Your grandfather slipped into a coma,
slipped away," she said,
while my thoughts focused on my need
to let go.

                    When my aunt's suffering was over
I looked at her body and closed my eyes
to remember her face, not the years
of surgery and chemistry,
of radiation focused through her
pain to keep her with us,
that slow separation of mind and body
healers hold so dear.

"I'm sorry about her," my husband said.
But I was crying over him.

                    In late spring
my losses followed the circuit of blood
from brain to heart, no possible splitting left
of the truth from what I felt
could leave me the familiar life,
with everyone alive and well.

In the Belly

Earrings, like a pair of wedding gloves:

a young clerk in the old world sells me white stones
from the window display. *Amber,* she intones,

and repeats, *amber.* Neither luminescent
fault-spiked caramel nor silent,

opaque coffee grounds, these crisp stars in night
sky draw my eye, my sight

slightly marbled by desire. I'm pondering another
I thought I'd lost like an old skin, a lover

set beside me in silver, to whom I was bound
and released, as from a watery deep brown.

I've climbed to err on autumn earth upon a crust
of papery leaves and spoken what I must,

yet conversations never end
when words wound inside begin

to surface through agents
like developing prints,

the way history seeps into the present hour
with purposes and meanings long turned sour.

A photograph appears darkest, tree
limbs serrating sky, where the negative is nearly

transparent. Chaos moves into form
while rigid design breaks like a maelstrom.

Beneath cathedrals, bridges, each grand structure
lies the grave of a worker,

a reversal. Where the world is torn
like a ticket, in the garden of betrayal worn

raw, I find the oldest amber
grown white and remember

the scars in the belly of love.

Sleeping Underground in a Krakow Park

Shade trees throw odd symmetries
of shadow to damp ground, where she
lays down her head, crown through the spine's
knots, to the trap of incarnation.

Teenaged boys mimic a crippled woman's
stumbling gait, but at least they are laughing,
I think, and we are safe, one woman asleep,
one sentinel awake. I see her shift,

my sleeping, younger self. Tangled in a cave
of sleep, she lays her body on the body of the map,
sinks stolid roots to Roman roads.
Plowing straight and deep, she covers the places

where we failed each other, by cinder and maul,
cannon, treaty, and marriage, covering
towns whose names still wound the tongue,
where no one sleeps with both eyes closed.

Sandstorm

We were only teenagers in pup tents,
Pitched on the outskirts of Zion,
Utah, along the Virgin River.

In 1974, we thought the war was over.
The summer night wrapped us
In its blaze, our gang lapped up
In one extravagant astral gesture.
Back east, never had we gazed
Into enlivened sky as fierce with stolen fire.

Our Promethean dreams came heavy-laden
As sacks of stone. Uneven ground
Beneath our thin foam beds
Brought ambiguous rest,
As we rolled to the Pacific west
In an old school bus, painted blue.

Something rose up from the south
That night in Zion, and gut-punched
Us while we slept or didn't. Over the border,
In Uzbekistan or Turkmenistan, exported sand-
Storms like these are known as "Afghans."

A force more fierce than wind alone
Sucked our structure of fragile aluminum
Until the forms, the dimensional spaces
Of our breathing, collapsed,
And we slashed through any opening, gasping.

The sky turned its back and tumbled
Into our mouths like blackened ash.
Arms outstretched, we tried our faulty reason
On the distance and the darkness
And the irrational, raging wind.

With all of the lights stripped
From the back of the sky, we tied our souvenir
T-shirts into face turbans to sift oxygen

From the sand that emblazoned our skin.
We walked blind, battered by haze,
Until our eyes stung, rid of illusions, until
Every one of our prayers had been undone
By the wilderness we had wanted to know.

We were just teenagers in pup tents,
Intent on experience, and *oh brother, goddamn,*
How it would find us, again and again, wherever we hid.

Koan

Of suffering,
she said,
I've little firsthand knowledge,
except my one attempt

to crush it like an ant
on a sunny pavement.
What oozed out
delighted me, she said.

A little child came
and tapped it with one foot
which stuck
fast as a snap to the spot.

Moving

On a train, an illusion of motion
seems real. When you are hanging out

the window, watching another train
leave the station,

you feel as though you are moving.
You cannot be sure which one

of you is slurring away or toward,
as each adjustment creates another,

and for every degree of distance opening
or closing, there enters a ghost,

a note held too long in the mind
to be tuneful. You cannot tell whether

your train is moving or still. On a train,
waiting to hear the whistle, you hang

out the window, your lower half
claiming space in the compartment,

your rational octopus waving wildly
to the twin beside you on the tracks.

When and if you see your shadow move,
you are either the first mover

or the moon, mimicking its light,
but in the dark, we believe what we see.

This condition continues until the wheels
pick up momentum and one train

pulls away, taking everything
you ever dreamed was real.

Your House When You Are Gone

Clouds multiplied on the rectangles
of your eyes. The rectangles of your house

repeat in light—your whole habitation moves
in darkness and reflection. It is not something you

see but something you are, that in moving
over surfaces becomes you. The eye

of the house fits snug in the socket
of good-bye. I lie on your bed

and mold my body to your shadows, shadows
felt and shadows glimpsed at the corners

of my sight like winter sparrows,
common birds that still take flight.

I sleep fitful in hallways and kitchen—
like a tight suit, your house when you

are gone hands me down to itchy, threadbare
silence. I try on silence

like clothes that bear your scent. The windows
of your house are too small for the sky

when you are gone. The rooms
split, walls from ceilings, unfold,

infer. Nothing but the shattering left.
I am lying on the bed that sinks

into a river. Water moves over me now
down to the mouth. All tributaries wash out.

The windows are too small for the sky in this house.

Feeding the Birds

Small motions call me into service
on a frozen day. When white-breasted nuthatches,
slate juncos, and jays nibble the last seed,

I go out into the falling ice
to fill the feeders, forgetting
gloves and hat, so that my fingers

bloom like tulips and ache.
The doggerel of sustained bad weather,
none too clever the first time,

repeats its recitation, predictable
schemes, mixed in with the noise of past
sins and sleet on the roof.

My mind wanders toward hot chocolate
as toward someone I fully remember
but have yet to know. Each love

enfolds every other, the way
scents of chocolate pull me into
the kitchen with Mother mixing icing

for the cake left to cool on the counter.
I awaited her offer, sticking close
to each small motion of her hands.

I never learned to ask for what I wanted,
depending on my mother's love
of chocolate, daring to hope she'd notice me.

Now I pour steaming cocoa for myself alone.
Outside the window birds scatter seed as though
nothing were scarce or limited by what I know.

Iris Apologia

I offer you these irises
Snipped from their roots
To bloom briefly.

I hand over this heart,
Which like a hawk
Has worn its taming hood.

From my armor I strip
But not to dress in your colors
Or convince you of my honor.

I discard the bargain basement
Hair shirt mollification
Inspired me to don—

Its hypocritical dimensions
Hemmed us both in, darling.
And finally, I release

The lovely lead weights
From my dancing feet—
Entangled with your fears

These tripped me up no end.
Your plumage, its rare flights
And raving beauty,

Your sweet aviary
Of competing
Song completes me.

Wonder

Her neck tastes of apples.
In this kitchen, chocolate

pours into tin fish.
The moment the wind lifts

fine hair above her ear,
I see her make a decision.

Slurring tires and then nothing.
I stall in a snow drift.

Over the barbed wire
I toss the car!

This is my dream, I am thinking,
I can do anything.

Poem for the Pardoned

From hypoblast to this acknowledgment:
no one knows why

the strange just keep on breathing. I
am wondering about the pardoned

and the condemned, one Sunday afternoon,
peering through the pollen-smeared windows

of my glass house in the woods. After winter
queries and postcards bearing quips,

Just be somewhere, I tell myself.
Even in a cell,

behind bars, there's a sense of belonging.
I know that

every kiss burns a question mark into the skin's
recall. I know that

every birdsong I hear can't be serious.
I think I'll answer as my dying aunt once did

if anyone asks,
"What have you been doing?"

I've been being, she said.
I laughed,

hurrying out the door to a film.
Now I see her perfection.

Forgiveness

A zeppelin roused
by a zephyr
      lifts:

weight so long attached
it's easy to forget
why shoulders hitch,

why back, bereft,
hunched under habit, rejects
this light experience.

Trust a breath
      ajar
in indigent, smoky space.

Do not defeat this gift,
      this loss
of anchoring regret.

Buddha Going out of Business

Buddha balances in the backseat
of the jeep, shoulder-harnessed,
and for good measure,
childproof locked. I drive through
the bank, make a deposit.

Buddha cost twenty-one dollars
plus odd change, not much
for a plaster-cast, bronze-painted
incarnation. I waited a week
for the final markdown,

worried that I'd miscalculate
this moment. But now I'm happy,
so happy, with my Buddha.
I drive through for burgers,
one with cheese, one without.

I curb my Buddha, chew burgers because
my last lover eschewed meat and lied.
Alone with my balancing,
balancing Buddha, I think:
This is the best of lives.